Ultimate Large Print Dot-to-Dot For Adults
Extreme Stress Relieving Puzzles
Puzzles From 150 to 726 Dots

By Laura's Dot to Dot Therapy

Copyright © 2018

All rights reserved. No part of this publication may be reproduced, distributed, or transmitted in any form or by any means, including photocopying, recording, or other electronic or mechanical methods, without the prior written permission of the publisher

How To Use This Book

Hi! We're so glad you're a lover of puzzles and dot connecting- we are too!

Connecting the dots in this book is simple- just relax and follow the numbers in consecutive order, drawing a straight line between each one. Dot 1 will connect to dot 2 and so on and so forth until there are no more dots to connect. There's always another dot and you'll always find it. Connect every dot to discover the beautiful images they create.

In case you get lost or can't find a dot, never stress- there's an answer key at the back of the book that will show you exactly where each dot connects to the next. If you want to color your images, we encourage you to do so! Feel free to try all different colors and coloring mediums for your images!

If you find any errors or omissions in this book, email us at Laurasdottodot@gmail.com and please let us know! We want you to have the best dot to dot experience!

Page 2

Page 3

Page 10

Page 13

Page 15

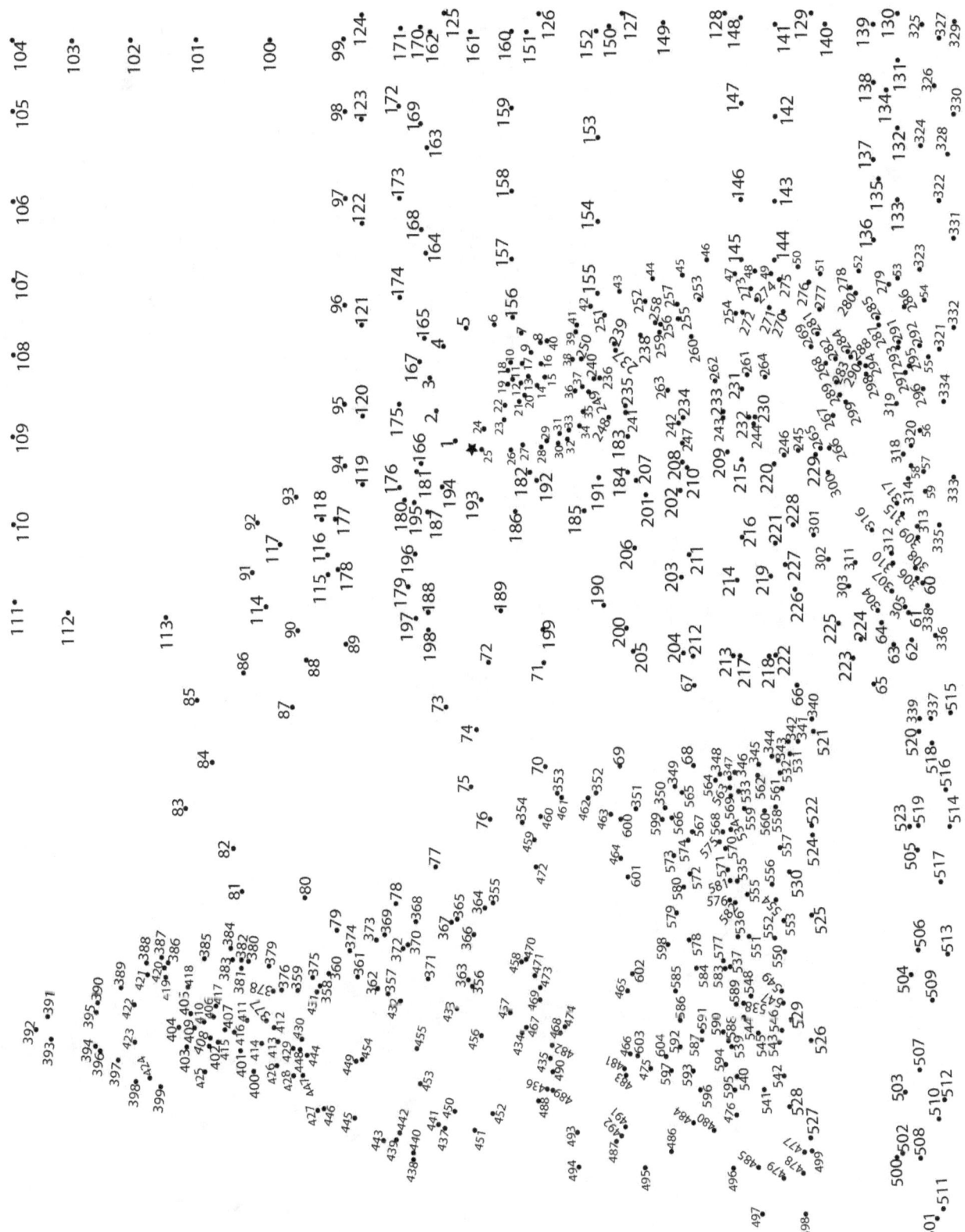

Enjoy bonus images from some of our other fun dot-to-dot books

Find all of our books on Amazon

Antique Cars and Vintage Cars
Large Print Dot-to-Dot Book for Adults

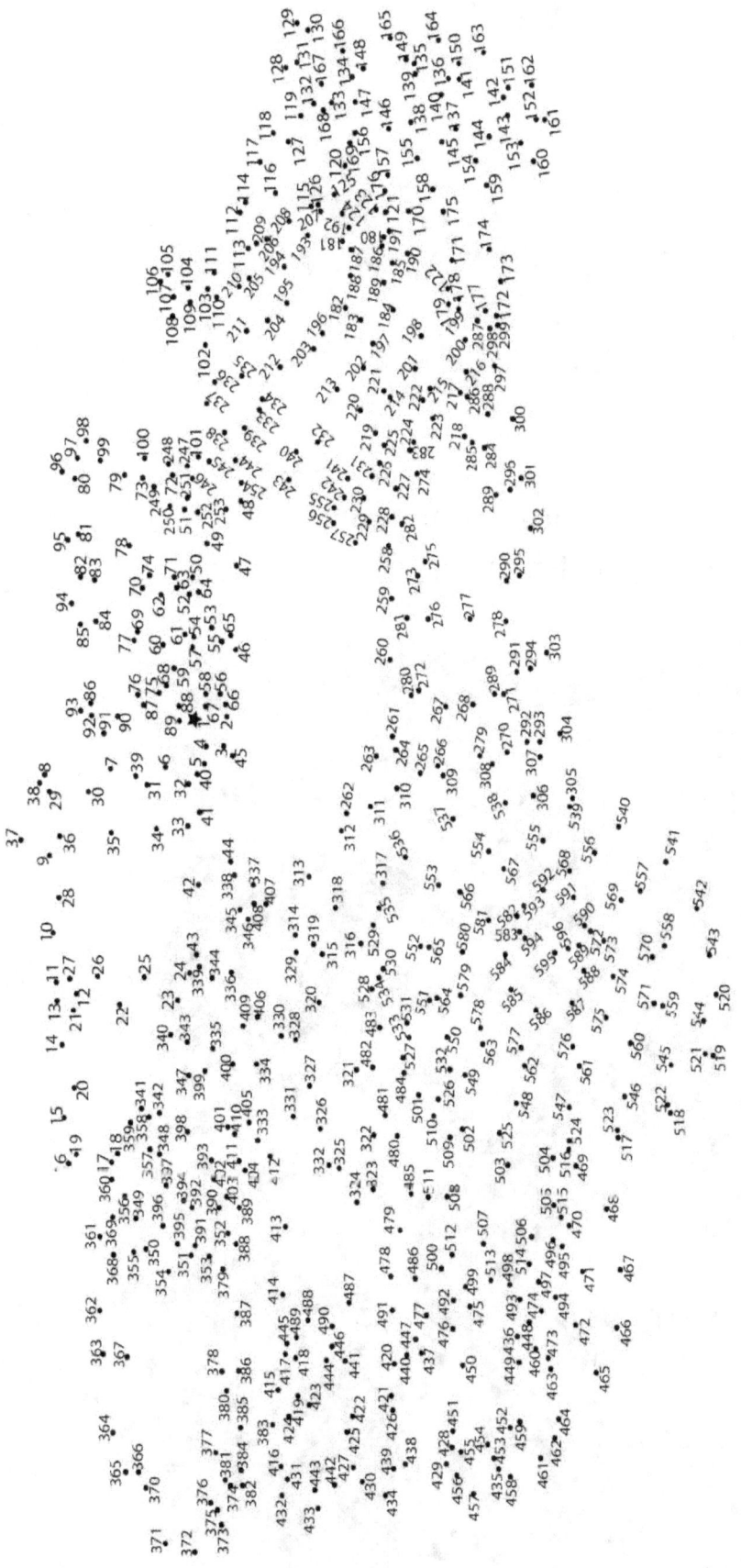

Famous Faces
Big Book of Extreme Dot to Dot

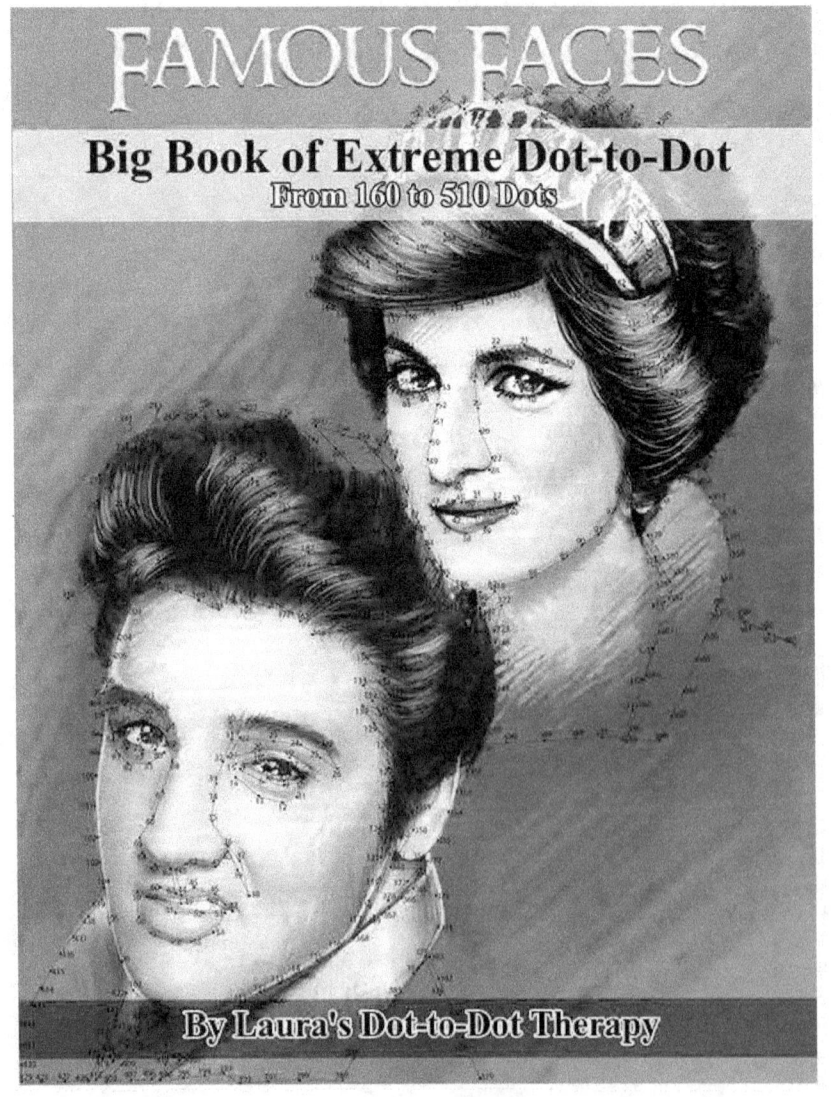

Mythical Mermaid
Dot-to-Dot Book for Adults
Puzzles from 150 to 750 Dots

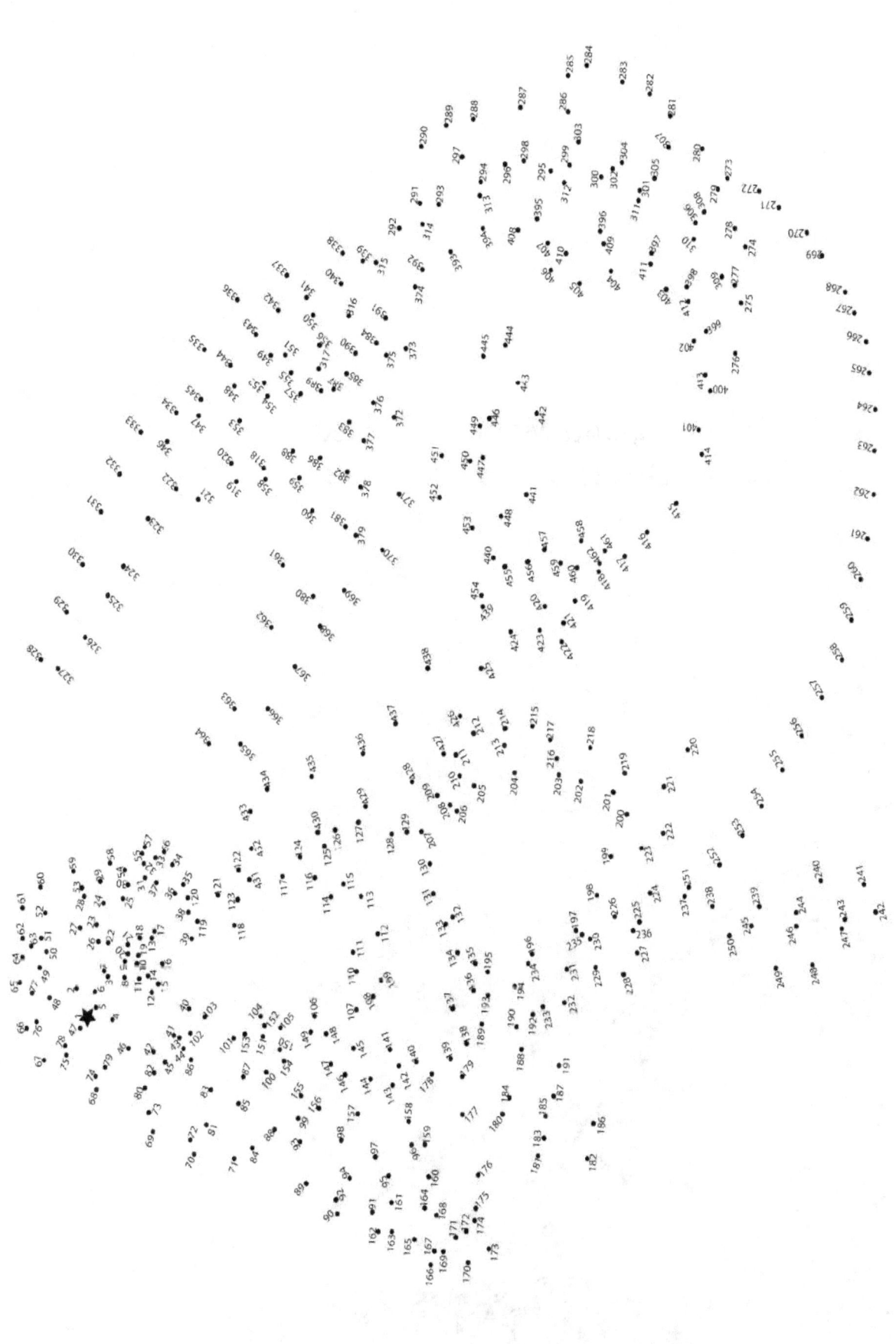

Unicorn, Dragons, and Magical Creatures
Dot-to-Dot Puzzles from 462 to 956 Dots

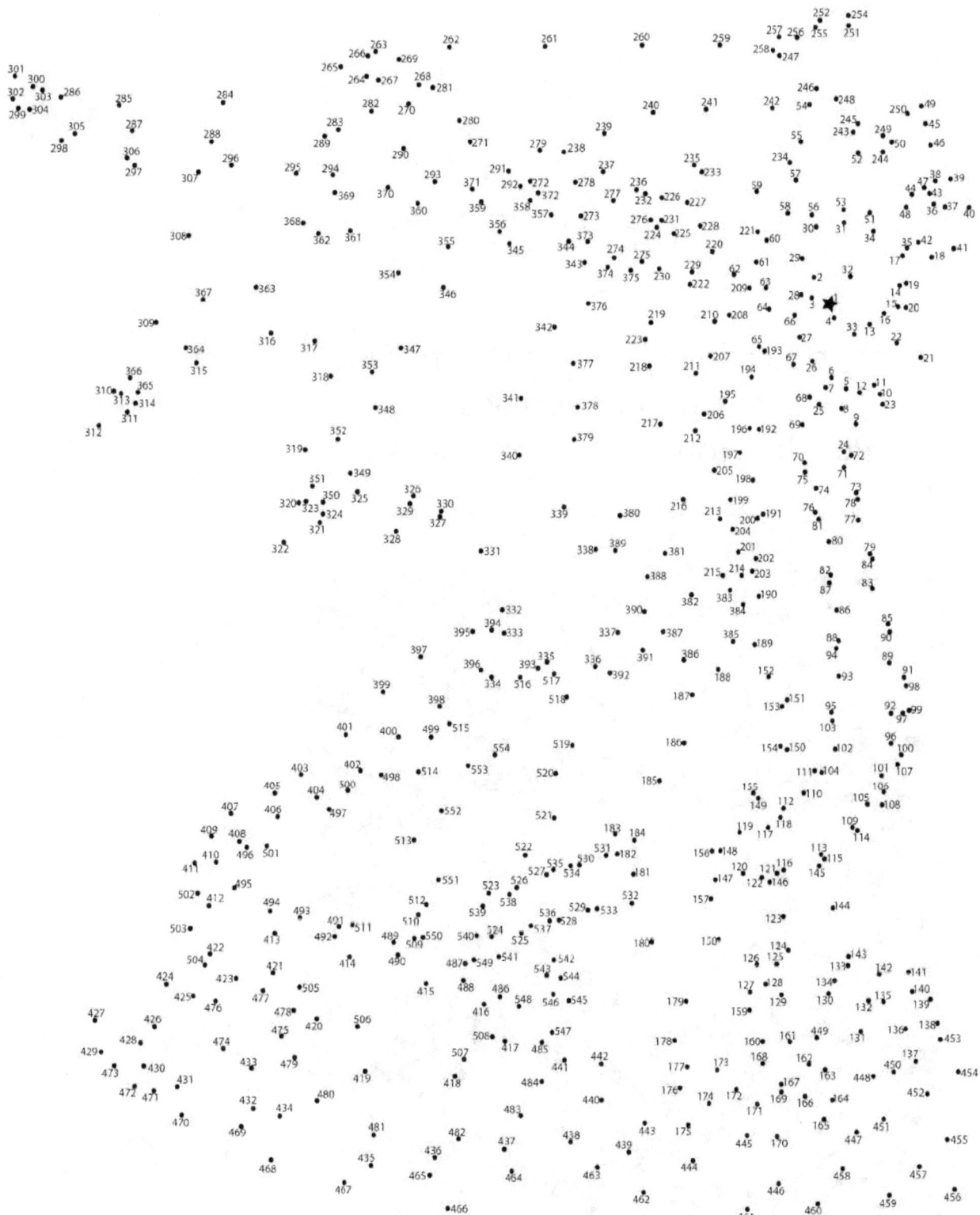

Easy to Read Large Print Dot to Dot
Beautiful Landscapes
Puzzles from 150 to 760 Dots

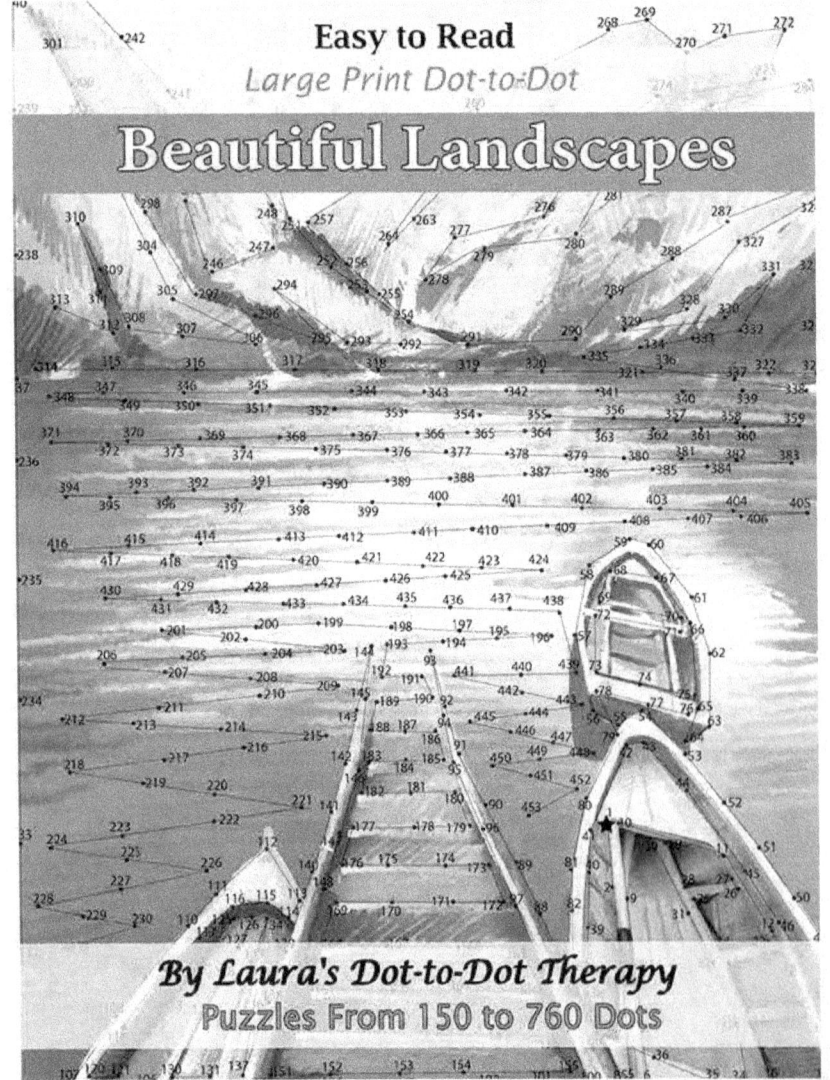

Answer Key

Follow along with the page numbers from top left to bottom right

Page 17

Page 18

Page 19

Page 20

www.ingramcontent.com/pod-product-compliance
Lightning Source LLC
Chambersburg PA
CBHW081627220526
45468CB00009B/2327